MW01167245

© 1995 The Government of Ireland

Written by Edel Bhreathnach and
Conor Newman, The Discovery Programme.

Photography (unless otherwise stated) Con Brogan,
John Swan (helicopter pilot).

Artefact Illustrations (unless otherwise stated) Joe Fenwick.

Calligraphy Denis Brown.

Design Creative Inputs.
Separations by Lithographic Plate Plan Ltd.
Printed by Turners Printing

The authors wish to acknowledge the assistance of the following
individuals and institutions:

Joe Fenwick and Kieron Goucher, The Discovery Programme;
Prof. George Eogan, Dr. Eoin Grogan, Dr. Séamus Caulfield, Prof.
Barry Raftery, Fionnbar Moore, Gerard Clarke, The Royal Irish
Academy, The National Museum of Ireland, The National Library
and Trinity College Dublin.

ISBN 0-7076-1695-6

Published by the Stationery Office

To be purchased through any Bookseller or directly from
Government Publications Sales Office, Sun Alliance House,
Molesworth Street, Dublin 2.

£3.00

Contents

preface

This Guide stems from the major research initiative that is being carried out by the Discovery Programme into the archaeology and history of Tara and its environs. The role of the Discovery Programme is to enhance our understanding of Ireland's past through archaeological and related research. It is the policy of the Discovery Programme to disseminate new information to as wide an audience as possible at both popular and scholarly levels.

Tara of the Kings, celebrated in myth and legend, is one of Ireland's premier archaeological sites. Although the hill is not a prominent feature of the landscape, it commands panoramic views of the Irish countryside and of some of the richest and most fertile land in Ireland. Archaeology has established that human activity on the hilltop goes back to the Neolithic period, about five-and-a-half thousand years ago, while the earliest historical references to Tara can be dated to the seventh century AD. Despite all of this, the archaeological richness of Tara is often not apparent to the extent that one often hears the remark that there is very little to see on the Hill of Tara. This Guide introduces the visitor to the monuments and history of Tara.

The first part of the Guide deals with the literary and historical aspects of the site – the myths and legends of Tara, the kingship of Tara, its association with Saint Patrick and its pedigree as the symbolic capital of Ireland. The second part is concerned with the archaeological aspect of this royal site. There are over thirty visible monuments at Tara and as a result of the Discovery Programme's research, based on detailed topographic survey, geophysical prospection and aerial photography, as many again have been identified. The hill is, therefore, a mosaic of monuments, one of the richest archaeological complexes in Ireland.

It is hoped that this Guide will help to create a better understanding and appreciation of this notable site. Tara is not a mute hilltop, but a site that through its remains reflects the vibrant nature of this once great centre of activity.

George Eogan

Chairman,
The Discovery Programme

Introduction

William Wilde, the nineteenth-century antiquarian and father of Oscar Wilde, wrote a travel book on the river Boyne and its tributary, the Blackwater. On visiting Tara, his imagination, combined with a romantic view of the hill, could not be contained:

> Standing at the top or southern extremity of this remain, and bearing in mind the various prose and bardic histories of the Irish annalists, one cannot help reverting to ancient heroic times, and again, in imagination, peopling it with its early occupants. Here sat in days of yore kings with golden crowns upon their heads; warriors with brazen swords in their hands; bards and minstrels with their harps; grey-bearded ollamhs; druids with their oak-leaf crowns...

Tara, whose mysterious earthen mounds inspired this romantic view, is the place which popular belief associates with Celtic myth and legend. The unusual monuments lead the imagination to regard Tara as the home of gods and heroes, not of ordinary humans.

The earliest historical records in Ireland date to around the middle of the sixth century AD. There are references to Tara in documents of the seventh century, in poems, lives of Saint Patrick, annalistic records and king-lists. The symbolic importance of Tara and its fascination for early chroniclers has meant that there is a huge body of documentary material associated with it in the medieval period. This material combines myth, legend and historical fact, strands which are not always easily separated. One of the difficulties facing historians and archaeologists is assessing the relevance of the pseudo-historical and mythological material to the prehistoric period, when most of the monuments at Tara were built.

Late Bronze Age sword from near Tara.

the Setting

The Hill of Tara lies about midway between the towns of Dunshaughlin and Navan in the gently rolling countryside of south central Meath. The monuments comprising the Tara complex are scattered along a low ridge about 2km long, a little to the west of and parallel to the main road. Unimposing from the east, the ground rises steadily to about 155m above sea level before dropping away quite steeply to the west presenting a spectacular vista over the Central Plain of Ireland. This aspect was a deciding factor in the choice of this hill as a ritual and political focus. Prominent heights are often regarded as the meeting places of the sacred and the profane, of man and the gods and in providing views of other elevated ritual complexes they promote the notion of a community of intervisible sacred places – tombs, cairns and hillforts.

The southern horizon is dominated by the Dublin and Wicklow mountains where there are a number of Neolithic passage tomb cemeteries including Saggart Hill, Montpelier (the Hell-fire Club) and Seefin. To the northwest the horizon is defined by Slieve na Calliagh, near Oldcastle, County Meath, on the summits of which can be seen the passage tomb cemetery of Loughcrew. In the middle distance, a little further to the north is the monastic town of Kells and behind it the Hill of Lloyd with its tower (built in 1791), also the site of a late prehistoric hillfort. Hidden from view below Kells is Teltown, where *Óenach Tailten*, presided over by the king of Tara, was held periodically. It was the most famous of the assemblies dedicated to the Celtic god Lug, and one which later continued as a harvest festival. Slieve Gullion, in south Armagh, defines the northern horizon and it too is topped by a large cairn. To the northeast are the Mountains of Mourne forming a spectacular backdrop to the Cooley mountains in County Louth, setting for the great epic *Táin Bó Cúailnge* ('Cattle Raid of Cooley'). Due east, and considerably closer, is the Hill of Skreen with the ruins of a medieval parish church with its prominent bell-tower and to the south of this Fourknocks Hill, site of another important passage tomb cemetery.

Tara from the northwest.

Tara from the South.

The greatest concentration of monuments is on and around the summit of the hill. It is clear, however, from the number of outlying monuments in the surrounding countryside, such as those known as Rath Meave to the south and Rath Lugh to the east, that Tara belongs to a much wider complex of related ritual and settlement sites. The idea that five great roadways radiated from Tara is repeated in a number of early tales. One tale relates how five roads, Slige Midlúachra, Slige Asail, Slige Chualann, Slige Dála and Slige Mór, appeared magically to mark the birth of Conn Cétchathach, a mythical king of Ireland. The routes of these roads can be partly followed throughout Ireland. A number of disused roads converge at Tara, but their antiquity cannot be verified to the extent of relating them with the five mythological roadways of Tara.

Rath Maeve.
A large henge at the southern end of the Tara complex.

Although the boundary between sacred and profane is at best ill-defined, there can be no doubting the ritual primacy of Tara: it was the focus of collective ritual and ceremony in this area.

Some of the principal prehistoric sites around Tara.

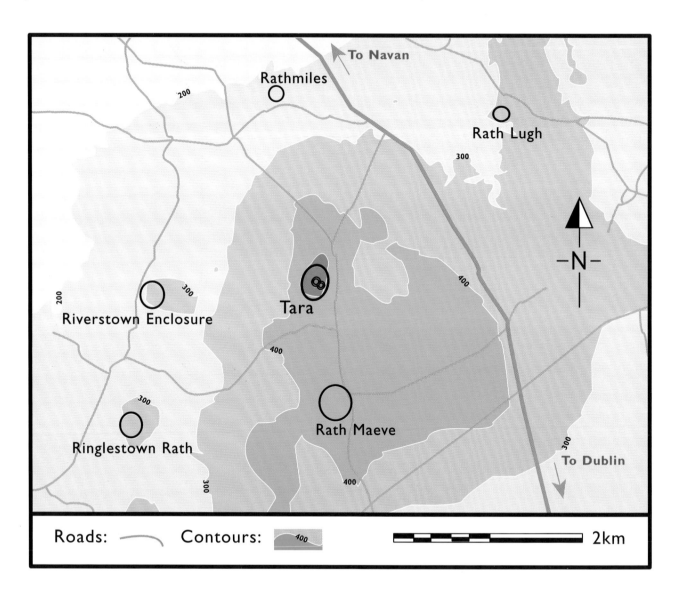

Roads: Contours: 400   2km

The Name Temair (Tara)

The ninth-century text *Sanas Cormaic*, a glossary attributed to the king-bishop of Cashel Cormac mac Cuilennáin who died in 908 AD, provides two explanations for the Irish name *Temair*. The first explanation is that *Temair* derived from *tea-múr*, the wall (*múr*) of Tea, the wife of Eirimón, a mythological king of Tara. It is related that Tea died at Tara homesick for her native Thebes in Egypt and was buried on the hill. The other explanation is that the word *Temair* means a height from which there is a fine view, a derivation possibly influenced by the natural setting of the hill. These may not be the true origins of the name, but rather folk explanations. The real meaning may have to do with ideas of twilight and darkness, perhaps a sacred space or 'the gates to the otherworld' – a concept also enshrined in the Greek place-name *Pylos*. The anglicized version of *Temair*, Tara, appears to have originated from the form *Taueragh* current during the thirteenth century, as it is recorded in Anglo-Norman documents.

A page of the dinnshenchas from the Book of Ballymote.

Courtesy Royal Irish Academy.

Myth and Legend

Tara is portrayed in the earliest Irish sagas as the domain of gods and goddesses and heroic, semi-divine kings. It is seen as the centre of an ancient sacral kingship, the seat of priest-kings. Whatever the truth of this belief, and it should be remembered that these are sagas and not historical accounts, the early descriptions of the gods and kings of Tara are highly colourful and fanciful.

Iron Age stone heads, representing Celtic gods or goddesses.

The Gods and Goddesses of Tara

Tara was inhabited by otherworldly beings, the most important of whom were the god Lug and the goddess Medb. Lug is the greatest of the Celtic gods. He is the divine manifestation of the kingship of Tara, the ancestor deity of Tara, whose voice was heard through the utterances of the Lia Fáil. He is the *samildánach* or omnicompetent god. His arrival at Tara is described in the ninth-century text *Cath Maige Tuired* ('The Battle of Moytura'). He arrives unannounced at Tara wearing the crown of a king and leading a band of strangers. The doorkeeper, who does not recognise him, asks Lug what art he practices, for none without an art may enter Tara. Lug lists various skills, the doorkeeper rejecting them one by one. Finally, Lug tells the doorkeeper to go to Nuadu, the king of Tara and to ask him if he has a single man who is skilled in all these arts. Nuadu admits that there is no such person in Tara. Lug enters Tara and Nuadu rises before him, recognizing him as the new king of Tara.

15

Lug had the power to legitimise a man's authority as king of Tara. What type of ceremony was devised to symbolise Lug's granting of authority on a king of Tara is not documented historically. The text, *Baile in Scáil* ('The Phantom's Vision'), which dates in part to the ninth century, describes Lug acting as a prophet foretelling the names of the kings of Tara which belong to the dynasty of the north and midlands of Ireland, the Uí Néill. He directs a beautiful young girl, probably in origin the goddess of sovereignty, to dispense drink from a golden cup to Conn Cétchathach, a mythological ancestor of the Uí Néll dynasty.

The sóvereignty of Tara in its female manifestation is symbolised by the goddess Medb. Medb, whose name is associated with intoxication, could also legitimise the reign of a king of Tara, often by offering him an intoxicating drink and by sleeping with him, symbolising the rite of fertility and the union between the king and his land. In the absence of a suitable candidate for the kingship of Tara, Medb on occasion ruled Tara herself until the rightful king was found. The goddess could appear in the form of a hag, as she did to the ancestor of the Uí Néill, Níall Noígiallach ('Niall of the Nine Hostages') and his brothers. An eleventh-century tale *Echtra mac nEchdach Mugmedóin* ('The Adventures of the sons of Eochaid Mugmedón') relates how of all the sons of Eochaid Mugmedón, Níall alone agreed to kiss the hag. By doing so, he was granted the sovereignty of Tara and the hag was transformed into a beautiful young woman.

The Heroic Kings of Tara

The kingship of Tara was based on the universal concepts of kings ruling justly, peacefully, prosperously and truthfully. Early Irish texts on kingship incorporate these ideals into one phrase, *fír flathemon*, 'the justice of a ruler'. The fortunes of the two great legendary kings of Tara, Conaire Mór and Cormac mac Airt, depend on how well they adhered to these ideals. Both kings, whose historical existence is doubtful, are a fusion of god and man and their lives reflect this duality.

Two gold torcs found at Tara in 1810

According to legend, Conaire Mór begins his reign when he overcomes the ordeals awaiting anyone who aspired to be king of Tara. These ordeals are described in an eighth-century text *De Shíl Chonairi Moir* ('Of the Race of Conaire Mór'):

There was a king's chariot at Tara. To the chariot were yoked two horses of the same colour, which had never before been harnessed. It would tilt up before any man who was not destined to receive the kingship of Tara, so that he could not control it, and the horses would spring at him. And there was a king's mantle in the chariot. He who was not destined to enjoy the sovereignty of Tara the mantle was much too big for him. And there were two stones in Tara: 'Blocc' and 'Bluigne'; when they accepted a man, they would open before him until the chariot went through. And Fál was there, the 'stone penis' at the head of the chariot-course; when a man should have the kingship of Tara, it screeched against his chariot-axle, so that all might hear. But the two stones Blocc and Bluigne would not open before one who should not hold the sovereignty of Tara, and their usual position was such, that one's hand could only pass sideways between them; also he who was not to hold Tara's kingship, the Fál would not screech against his axle.

Photo: Courtesy National Museum of Ireland

17

The Lia Fáil

Whether it is real or imaginary, this account evokes the array of symbols associated with the kingship of Tara. There are the stones Blocc and Bluigne which appear elsewhere in the guise of druids. Lia Fáil is the stone which is reputed to have cried out on recognising a man as the king of Tara. The author is likely to have had the Tech Midchúarta (Banqueting Hall) at Tara in mind when he referred to the chariot-course. It is clear that the underlying theme of the description is that of fertility which symbolised the reign of a righteous and successful king.

The concept of truth, part of the ideal kingship, is associated particularly with the recognition of the heroic Cormac mac Airt as king of Tara. According to this tale, Cormac enters Tara and is confronted by a woman complaining about a judgement meted out to her by the reigning king of Tara, Lugaid mac Con. Her sheep have been forfeited by Lugaid for grazing in the queen's woad field. Cormac declares that this is a false judgement – the correct verdict being that one shearing of the sheep's wool would be a proper fine for the loss of one year's harvest. This judgement of truth led to Cormac being recognised as the rightful king of Tara. Lugaid's false judgement forced him to abdicate and caused one side of his royal house to collapse, thereby explaining the unusual shape of the Clóenfherta or 'Sloping Trenches'.

There are no descriptions of actual inaugurations held at Tara. The assembly at Tara, *Feis Temro*, may have been some form of fertility rite held at the height of a particularly successful king's reign. Celebration of the event seems to have stopped in the sixth century when the kings of Tara accepted Christianity.

The kings of Tara were supposed to have been bound by taboos, many of them fantastical and more likely the imaginings of later men of learning. A description of the taboos associated with the reign of Conaire Mór, which are as colourful as those of the ordeals awaiting him before he is recognised as king of Tara, are incorporated into the ninth-century text *Togail Bruidne Da Derga* ('The Destruction of Da Derga's Hostel'):

He could not pass Tara on his right hand and Brega [a territory comprising modern county Meath and parts of counties Dublin and Louth] on his left; he could not hunt the crooked beasts [swans] of Cernae [possibly Carnes, near Duleek, County Meath]; he could not stay away from Tara for longer than nine days; he could not spend the night in a house in which firelight was visible outside after sunset and into which a person could see from outside; three red men could not go before him into a red man's house; plunder could not be undertaken during his reign; a visiting party consisting of one man or one woman could not come into his house after sunset; he could not settle a quarrel between two of his subjects.

Iron Age horsebit from the valley between Tara and Skreen.
Illustration courtesy of Prof. Barry Raftery and the National Museum of Ireland.

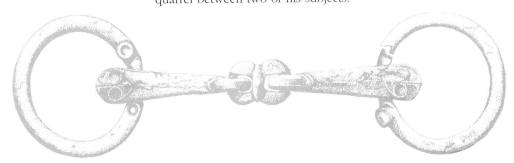

The Kingship of Ireland

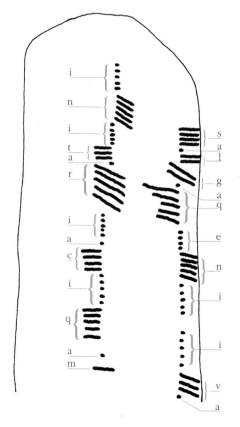

Tara is often regarded as the seat of the high-kings of Ireland. This popular belief has its origins primarily in the literary creations of medieval historians from the seventh century onwards. Wishing to promote their own political and ecclesiastical aspirations, they sought to institute the idea of a national monarchy, although it is unlikely that this was a reality until at least the ninth century. The kings of Tara were different from other kings in Ireland and any king who succeeded in gaining the title *rí Temro*, 'king of Tara', in the early historic period must have been accorded some special status. This title implied dominance over other kings, but it did not necessarily reflect a territorial claim over the whole island.

An ogham inscription from Painestown, County Meath (about 11km to the northeast of Tara) commemorating a Leinster king, Mac Cairthainn, reputed to have been king of Tara.

(Illustration courtesy of Fionnbar Moore)

The Early Historic Kings of Tara

The earliest references to historic kings of Tara are preserved in documents which date primarily to the seventh century. These early texts tell of a kingship which was a source of contention in the fifth, sixth and seventh centuries between rival dynasties from Leinster, Ulster, the northwest and the midlands (the northern and southern Uí Néill).

Ireland c. 700 AD.

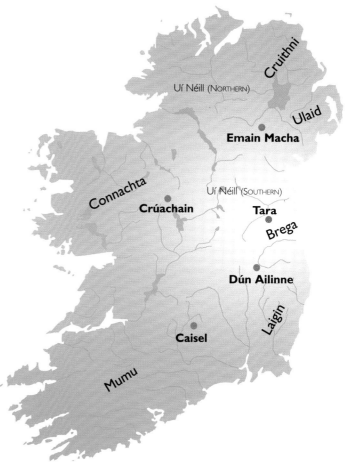

The claims of kings of Leinster (a province which in early historic times extended little beyond Tara) to have held the kingship of Tara are echoed in early poems which proclaim the origins and glory of Leinster. One poem calls on the Leinstermen not to forget that they once held the kingship of Tara and lists Leinster kings who, according to this tradition, ruled Tara as far back as the late fourth and fifth centuries AD.

The next phase in this early contention for the kingship of Tara involves the Ulaid and the Uí Néill. The clearest reference to kings of the Ulaid claiming the kingship of Tara is contained in the early Irish laws. The seventh-century law-tract on bees, *Bechbretha*, tells how Congal Cáech lost the kingship of Tara because he was blinded by a bee sting. A king with a blemish could not continue to rule. Congal Cáech was king of the Cruithin of Ulster who was killed in 637 at the battle of Mag Rath (Moira, County Down) at the hands of the Uí Néill king, Domnall mac Áedo.

The Uí Néill succeeded in dominating Tara, both politically and conceptually, from the seventh century. They consisted of a confederation of dynasties who emerged in the fifth century AD to control the northern half of Ireland. They, and the men of learning who supported their cause, promoted the already important kingship of Tara into a national institution which they claimed had been the preserve of the Uí Néill. The biographer of Saint Patrick, Muirchú, writing about 680, describes Tara as *caput Scotorum*, 'the capital of the Irish', thus indicating that Tara had already achieved a national status. The king-list, *Baile Chuinn* ('The Vision of Conn'), relates in the form of a prophecy the names of the kings of Tara from Conn Cétchathach to Fínsnechta Fledach (died 695). This list deliberately omits the claims of certain dynasties, such as of the Leinster and Ulster kings, to Tara. This propaganda advanced the notion that the Uí Néill were the rightful heirs of this special kingship.

The symbolic importance of Tara as a ritual centre survived the adoption of Christianity in Ireland. Óengus, who compiled a calendar of saints around 830, proclaimed:

> The strong fortress of Tara has perished
> with the death of her princes;
> with its choirs of wisemen
> great Armagh lives on.

Though this dramatic description of the abandonment of Tara has been quoted as evidence of its desolation by the ninth century, this is not borne out by other records. The Columban community of Raphoe, County Donegal, came to Tara to curse the king of Tara, Áed Oirdnide, in 817 in revenge for his killing of the head of their church. The inference of this action is that Tara's symbolic associations drew the community of Raphoe there in order to confirm their curse on the king.

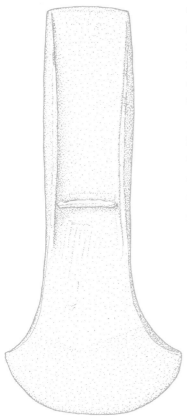

Bronze palstave from Tara.

The High Kingship of Ireland

The political and territorial primacy of Tara appears to have become a reality in the ninth century. The Irish chronicles known as the Annals of Inisfallen and the Annals of Ulster record that in 840 the astute king of Munster, Feidlimid mac Crimthainn, proved his domination of the midland regions of Brega and Mide by halting at Tara. There appears to have been less political fragmentation in Irish society from the ninth century onwards and power rested increasingly in the hands of a smaller number of kings. The Uí Néill king Máel Sechnaill I, who died in 862, could be regarded as the first king of Tara to control other provinces – a possible high-king of Ireland. His son, Flann Sinna, regarded himself as holding such as position when he had an inscription dedicated to himself, styled as RIG HERENN, 'king of Ireland', carved on the Cross of the Scriptures at Clonmacnoise, CountyOffaly.

The title *rí Temrach*, 'king of Tara', as the most powerful king in Ireland was replaced gradually by the title *rí Érenn*, 'king of Ireland'. More grandiose titles such as that describing the Munster king, BrianBorú as *imperator Scotorum*, 'emperor of the Irish', were also used. Although Tara's symbolic status increased from the eleventh century onwards, the title *rí Temrach* came to signify that of a

The Cross of the Scriptures, Clonmacnoise depicting Flann Sinna, king of Ireland, and abbott Colmán of Clonmacnoise.

local petty king. BrianBorú's rival, Máel Sechnaill II, who died in 1022, seems to have used the skills of his court poet, Cúán úa Lothcháin, to boost the symbolic importance of Tara. Úa Lothcháin is the reputed author of the topographical texts on the notable natural and man-made features of Ireland known as *Dinnshenchas Érenn* ('The Placelore of Ireland'). Tara takes precedence in the sequence of places covered in the *dinnshenchas*. The detailed account of the monuments at Tara in this topographical material is sufficient to regard it as a medieval survey of the hill.

Records of historic events taking place at Tara during this period are scant. The most notable exception is that of the battle of Tara in 980 in which Máel Sechnaill II defeated the Norse of Dublin and the Isles.

Máel Sechnaill II's death signalled the collapse of his dynasty, the southern Uí Néill. Tara and the kingdom of Mide lost out to Dublin in the eleventh century, because control of that city was essential to any king who aspired to rule the country and was more important than any link with a mythological kingship of Tara. Nonetheless, Tara appears in the literature of the eleventh and twelfth centuries, and increasingly in

Photo: Courtesy the National Museum of Ireland.

Part of the incription on the Shrine of the Stowe Missal which reads: OR DO DONDCHAD MACC BRIAIN DO RIG HEREND - 'A prayer for Donnchadh, son of Briain, for the King of Ireland'.

later literature, as a symbol of strength, nobility and legitimacy of power. The *Leabhar Gabhála* ('Book of Invasions'), a twelfth-century text which tells of the mythological invasions of Ireland by peoples from overseas who were the ancestors of the great kings of Ireland, describes the high-kingship as an ancient institution in existence from time immemorial.

Bardic poets used Tara to legitimize the authority of native and Anglo-Norman lords. The poet Gofraidh Fionn Ó Dálaigh (died 1387) likened the visit of Maurice Fitzmaurice (Muiris Óg), second earl of Desmond (died 1358) to London to the god Lug's visit to Tara. The seventeenth-century scholar and historian Geoffrey Keating (died 1649) strengthened the idea of Tara as the location of a national institution functioning from prehistoric times in his history of Ireland *Foras Feasa ar Éirinn*.

Early Bronze Age flat axe from Jordanstown, near Tara.

Saints and their Biographers

The most renowned episodes relating to Tara are found in the lives of saints. They are dramatic incidents, usually with an element of ecclesiastical or political propaganda, and they have influenced greatly subsequent views of the early history of Tara.

Patrick

Most notable among the descriptions of saints at Tara is the account of the confrontation between Patrick and Lóegaire, king of Tara and his druids:

It so happened in that year that a feast of pagan worship was being held, which the pagans used to celebrate with many incantations and magic rites and other superstitious acts of idolatry. There assembled the kings, nobles, leaders, princes, and the nobles of the people; furthermore, the druids, fortune-tellers, and the inventors and teachers of every craft and every skill were also summoned to king Loegaire at Tara, their Babylon, as they had

Medieval depiction of Saint Patrick, Rathmore, County Meath.

The Hill of Slane with the ruins of a medieval monastery.

been summoned at one time to Nabcodonossor, and they held and celebrated their pagan feast on the same night on which holy Patrick celebrated Easter. They also had a custom, which was announced to all publicly, that whosoever, in any district, whether far or near, should have lit a fire on that night before it was lit in the king's house, that is, in the palace of Tara, would have forfeited his life.

This dramatic account of Saint Patrick lighting the Paschal fire on the Hill of Slane, in opposition to the fire being lit on the Hill of Tara by its king Lóegaire, of the saint's consequent clash with the druids and the king's conversion to Christianity, is contained in a biography of Patrick written in the seventh century by Muirchú moccu Machtheni. Muirchú's description of the events are influenced greatly by biblical descriptions. He compares Lóegaire with Nabcodonossor and equates Tara with Babylon. This episode influenced all subsequent accounts to the extent that Patrick's clash with the druids at Tara became – like the high-kingship of Tara – a national belief. Muirchú linked Patrick with Tara at a time when the great church at Armagh, whose patron was Patrick, was expending much energy on forging a strong alliance with the increasingly powerful Uí Néill dynasty, who were using Tara as a symbol of their authority. Armagh's claim to ecclesiastical supremacy in Ireland would have been assisted by the knowledge that its patron saint, Patrick, had converted Lóegaire, an early Uí Néill king of Tara, to Christianity. There is, however, no contemporary historic evidence to support the claim that Patrick ever visited Tara.

Rúadán of Lorrha

The abandonment of Tara is traditionally associated with the tale of Saint Rúadán of Lorrha, County Tipperary, and his cursing of Diarmait mac Cerbaill, king of Tara. The historical truth of this tale is as questionable as that of Patrick's visit to Tara. It was probably composed to explain the official adoption of Christianity by Diarmait mac Cerbaill (died 565), the last king of Tara to celebrate the old fertility rite, *Feis Temro.*

From the early medieval period, Tara's potency as a political symbol developed to the extent that by the seventeenth century its central position in Ireland is not alone emphasised, but is proclaimed as one of the basic concepts of the nation. A particular phenomenon relating to Tara, which appears in later centuries, is the tendency of those launching campaigns, violent or otherwise, to gather there. This custom is not necessarily proof of continuity of tradition from an earlier period, it is more an acknowledgement of Tara's position as a national and political symbol. The Annals of the Four Masters record that in 1539 O'Neill and O'Donnell met there prior to launching a campaign. A document entitled the 'Meath Depositions', which relates what befell the Protestant population of Meath (and Louth) in the rebellion of 1641, tells of a meeting of lords and gentry held at Tara, among them the Earl of Fingal and the Lord of Gormanston. The hill was later the focus of a skirmish during the rebellion of 1798 and the setting for Daniel O'Connell's most famous Monster Meeting that was held in August 1843 and reputedly attended by one million people.

Apart, however, from any historical resonances that may have been attached to Tara in later centuries, its original potency is rooted in the four thousand years during which it was a pagan burial ground and focus of ritual ceremony, a time in its development that can only be approached through archaeology.

A nineteenth-century view of Daniel O'Connell's Monster Meeting held at Tara in August, 1843.

archaeological Remains

Royal Sites

Tara is chief among the best known 'royal' sites of Ireland, including Dún Ailinne in Leinster, Crúachain in Connacht and Emain Macha in Ulster. It is at once a landmark and a vantage point. The barrows, mounds, conjoined circular earthworks and buildings, timber henges, linear embankments and sacred springs and marshes at these royal centres together make up prehistoric 'ritual landscapes' that have evolved, in part by accident and in part by design, over many centuries. Hand in hand is the creation of a mythology that is every bit as real and potent as the monuments themselves – nowhere more so than at Tara.

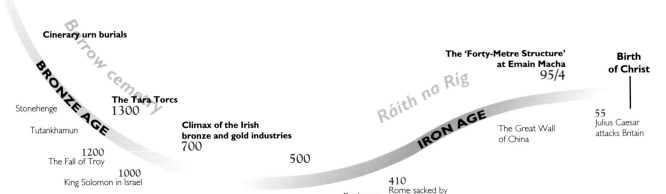

NEOLITHIC PERIOD

First agriculturalists
3800

First enclosure at Tara

The Boyne Valley Passage Tombs

The Mound of the Hostages

The Egyptian Pyramids

First metallurgists
2300

Beaker Pottery food vessel tradition

Cinerary urn burials

Barrow cemetery

BRONZE AGE

Stonehenge

Tutankhamun

The Tara Torcs
1300

1200
The Fall of Troy

1000
King Solomon in Israel

Climax of the Irish bronze and gold industries
700

500

Herodotus - the first mention of the Celts

Parthenon

410
Rome sacked by the Celts

Ráith na Ríg

IRON AGE

The Great Wall of China

The 'Forty-Metre Structure' at Emain Macha
95/4

Birth of Christ

55
Julius Caesar attacks Britain

Dún Ailinne,
seat of the Laigin of ancient
Leinster.

Crown copyright. Courtesy HMSO

Emain Macha,
seat of the Ulaid,
kings of Ulster.

Crúachain
the royal complex of ancient
Connacht.

Daniel O'Connell
meeting at Tara
1843

Publication of
George Petrie's paper on Tara
1839

French Revolution

Battle of Tara
1798

Battle of the Boyne
1690

Flight of the Earls
1603

Spanish Armada
1588

Dissolution of
the monasteries
1541

Columbus sails to
America
1492

Foundation of church at Tara
by Hospitallers of St. John
1230

The Black Death
1347

Arrival of Anglo-Normans
in Ireland
1169

Domnall úa Lochrainn,
king of Cenél nEógain at Tara
1104

First Crusade
1097

Battle of Hastings
1066

Battle of Clontarf
1014

First Irish coinage
997

The Battle of Tara
980

Founding of Dublin
841

899
Death of
Alfred the Great

Feidlimid mac Crimthainn
king of Munster at Tara
840

Book of Kells
800

First Viking raids
795

800
Coronation of
Emperor Charlemagne

Tara Brooch
700

NORMAN PERIOD

VIKING PERIOD

Church at Tara

rth of the Synods

Palladian mission to
minister Christians
in Ireland
431

Traditional date of
St. Patrick's arrival
432

Tech Cormaic

The last
celebration
of Feis Temro
560

Death of
Columba founder
of Iona
597

Roman conquest
of Britain

120
Hadrian's Wall

EARLY CHRISTIAN PERIOD

410
Collapse of Roman
Britain - Anglo-Saxon
invasion

453
Death of
Attila the Hun

Maya civilisation
pyramids in Mexico

622
Mohammed's flight
to Medina

Polished stone axehead from Kilmessan.

An examination of the surviving monuments tells us that the Hill of Tara was primarily a ritual site, a place where people came to bury their dead and where important events were celebrated by the community. It symbolised, authenticated and sustained the fabric of society. During the later prehistoric period it may have been guarded by the nearby fortified sites of Rath Lugh, Ringlestown Rath and Rath Miles. It may not have been until relatively late in its development that defence became a consideration at Tara itself. Ráith na Ríg, the major enclosure at Tara, like those at Dún Ailinne and Emain Macha, has its bank placed *outside* the ditch (or fosse), a patently non-defensive arrangement which appears to have had some special ritual significance. It has been suggested that the intention, rather than to deny access from without, was to contain a potent, otherworldly force. It is possible that the practice of using internally-ditched enclosures to define sacred space belongs to a long-standing tradition from the Late Neolithic to the Iron Age. It seems unlikely that there was ever a resident population at Tara in the prehistoric period and at times religious convention may have prevented anyone from living there at all.

There are over thirty visible monuments on the Hill of Tara and as many again that have no surface remains but which have been identified using geophysical prospection techniques and aerial photography. Most of the monuments on Tara can only be dated by comparison with others of known date elsewhere. Only two sites have been excavated, the Mound of the Hostages, one of the earliest monuments on Tara, and the Rath of the Synods which may be one of the latest. This gives a general time bracket for the monuments on Tara extending from the Neolithic (*c.* 3500 BC) to the later Iron Age (*c.* 400 AD). It is sometimes possible to establish a relative chronology for the monuments. For instance, the ramparts of Ráith na Ríg were laid out in such a way as to avoid the Mound of the Hostages, demonstrating that Ráith na Ríg is later.

The earliest monument so far identified is a large, probably palisaded enclosure around the summit of the hill that was built during the

Neolithic period. Part of this enclosure was found beneath the Mound of the Hostages. Only a few enclosures of this date are known from Ireland, e.g. at Knowth, County Meath and Lyles Hill, County Antrim, and although domestic activity is attested in some of them, in the majority of cases there is also evidence of ritual behaviour associated with death. Evidence from Britain suggests that Neolithic hilltop enclosures may have been used specifically for seasonal gatherings.

Most of the monuments at Tara are barrows - burial or funerary monuments consisting of a low earthen mound surrounded by a ditch and sometimes an outer bank. From the one hundred or so of these that have been excavated in Ireland it is evident that they remained in use from the Late Neolithic to the first few centuries after the birth of Christ. Although barrows cannot be dated on the basis of outward appearances alone, it is likely that the majority of those at Tara date to the Bronze Age. Time and erosion, agriculture and soil regeneration have reduced many of them to barely perceptible circles in the grass. There is a particular concentration of barrows along the northwestern and northern flanks of the hill, forming a small cemetery.

The Mound of the Hostages.

THE **MOUND OF THE HOSTAGES** takes its name from the medieval Irish designation of the monument Duma na nGiall, a name associating the monument with the symbolic exchange of hostages which must have taken place at Tara in the medieval period. It is, however, a passage tomb built around 3000 BC. The passage is 4m long and was divided by sillstones into three compartments, the floor of each formed by a large, flat slab. It is orientated roughly east – west with the entrance, which is flanked by two portal stones, facing east. One of the sidestones is decorated with concentric circles and zigzag patterns characteristic of passage tomb art. Although disturbed during the insertion of further burials during the Early Bronze Age, the assemblage of primary, Late Neolithic cremated burials and accompanying grave goods is one of the finest in the country.

This was a collective burial chamber probably receiving the cremated remains of the dead over many years. A layer of undisturbed primary burial deposits, 30cms deep, for instance, was found in the central compartment and was accompanied by the full range of artefacts normally associated with these tombs – including the distinctive passage tomb pottery (Carrowkeel Ware), bone pins, pendants and stone balls.

The Mound of the Hostages under excavation (1955).

Photo: OPW Photographic Archive

Some forty burials dating to the Early/Middle Bronze Age were found in the clay mantle covering the cairn of the passage tomb. These single burials signify a shift away from the collective burials of the earlier period and reflect the emergence of a more hierarchical social structure based on individual wealth. Although a number of inhumation burials of this period were placed in the passage, only one was found in the mantle of clay: all of the remaining burials were cremated. Many of these were contained under inverted cinerary urns which were in some cases accompanied by smaller Food Vessels and miniature pots. Some of the burials were contained in stone-built cists and in some cases two or more burials were placed in the same pit. The sole inhumation burial in the mound was that of a boy, about 14–15 years of age. Around the area of the neck were the remains of a necklace of jet, amber, bronze and faience beads and near the feet lay a small bronze knife and the very corroded remains of what may have been a bronze awl. That this youth was of privileged rank in society can be deduced from the exceptional grave goods, in particular the faience beads which may originate from the eastern Mediterranean and were a rare and exotic item in Bronze Age Ireland.

The decorated orthostat from the Mound of the Hosatages. The stone is decorated in typical passage tomb style with good parallels from Newgrange and Knowth. (Illustration: Joe Fenwick.)

Bronze Age urn burial from the Mound of the Hostages. Another burial contained a Collared urn and Vase Food Vessel, both of which were inverted, a rivetted bronze dagger and a polished stone battle axe, all evidently subjected to the intense heat of the funeral pyre.

Photo: OPW Photographic Archive

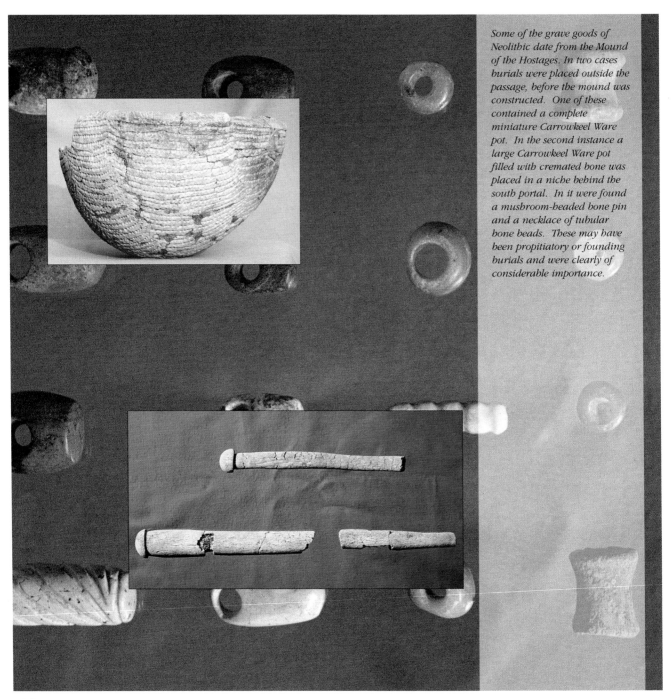

Some of the grave goods of Neolithic date from the Mound of the Hostages. In two cases burials were placed outside the passage, before the mound was constructed. One of these contained a complete miniature Carrowkeel Ware pot. In the second instance a large Carrowkeel Ware pot filled with cremated bone was placed in a niche behind the south portal. In it were found a mushroom-headed bone pin and a necklace of tubular bone beads. These may have been propitiatory or founding burials and were clearly of considerable importance.

Photo: Courtesy Department of Archaeology, University College Dublin.

36

RÁITH LÓEGAIRE commemorates in its name the early historic king of Tara, Lóegaire mac Néill, famous for his reputed clash with Patrick over the Paschal fire. Lóegaire is said to have been buried in the ramparts of Tara, facing his enemies, the Leinstermen. The monument, a circular enclosure about 130m in diameter, is one of the more problematical sites at Tara. The eastern half of the site has been erased by cultivation, but on the west side it is defined by a bank and internal ditch. There are, however, slight traces of an internal bank which, if original, and not simply the result of ploughing, suggest that the monument may have defensive characteristics. Geophysical survey has identified an entrance facing due east.

Ráith Lóegaire (foreground).

RÁITH NA RÍG, the Fort of the Kings, seems to have been given this name in the medieval period because of the royal associations with the monuments enclosed by it. These include Tech Cormaic, regarded as Cormac mac Airt's royal residence and the Forrad. The monument is a large ovoid enclosure. It is defined by an internal ditch and an external bank which is best preserved in the southwestern and northwestern quadrants. A section dug across the ramparts in 1953 revealed that the ditch, which was V-sectioned, was once an impressive 3.5m deep, most of which was cut into the shale bedrock. The stratigraphy recorded in the section is open to different interpretations, but it seems reasonably certain that a layer containing iron slag was sealed beneath the bank indicating that the ramparts were constructed during the Iron Age or later. The foundation trench for a wooden palisade was found running parallel to the ditch 2m inside it. This appears to have been a later addition and it had the effect of converting this ceremonial enclosure into a defensive one. Three entrances have been identified, in the south, east and northwest. It appears that the most important of these was the eastern one. None, however, is original and it seems that they are contemporary with the erection of the palisade. This may have signalled a dramatic departure in the function of the monument reflecting the demise of the old pagan order and the rise of the new Christian one where political expediency outweighed notions of pagan sanctity.

Ráith na Ríg in medieval descriptions is said to have enclosed three wonders, the Forrad, Tech Cormaic and Múr Tea. The Irish word *forrad* is likely to mean 'a mound or platform'. It is possible that the monument functioned as the location of inaugurations of kings of Tara.

Ráith na Ríg.

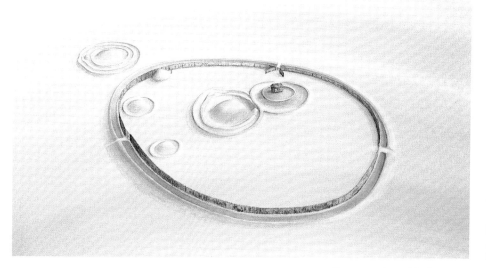

Reconstruction of the latest
phase at Ráith na Ríg.

Peter Monaghan

THE FORRAD and TECH CORMAIC consist of two conjoined earthworks. Tech Cormaic, regarded in the medieval period as being the royal residence of the heroic king of Tara, Cormac mac Airt, is a ringfort consisting of a circular area (about 70m in diameter) defined by two banks and an intervening ditch. The original entrance is in the northeast and is aligned, deliberately or otherwise, on the eastern entrance to Ráith na Ríg. Slightly off-centre is a low mound with a small hollow in the middle which may be the foundations of a house or perhaps the outline of a small barrow. Tech Cormaic is attached to the east side of the Forrad.

The Forrad and Tech Cormaic.

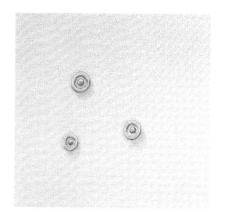 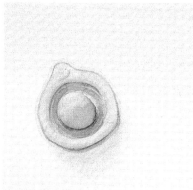 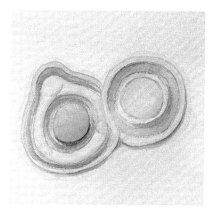

Peter Monaghan

The Forrad consists of a prominent, flat-topped mound surrounded by a ditch with two outer banks and an intervening ditch. It is possible to suggest three phases in its development. Before the present monument was built there may have been up to three small barrows here, arranged in the form of an equilateral triangle. When the large central mound and the middle bank were built the three barrows were incorporated into the bank. Two of them are clearly visible, one as a prominent protrusion in the northeastern quadrant, the second as a small round-topped mound in the southeastern quadrant. This may be *Múr Tea*, 'Tea's wall', the burial place of a mythical queen, described in the medieval account as being a little hillock located between the Forrad and Cormac's royal residence. The third is evidenced as a bulge or widening of the bank in the western quadrant. The outer bank is considerably narrower than the inner bank and appears to have been a later addition. It seems to be an extension of the outer bank of Tech Cormaic, the result, perhaps, of a deliberate attempt to associate this clearly important burial complex with the later habitation site.

Suggested sequence in the development of the Forrad and Tech Cormaic. In a number of instances, pre-existing monuments, in recognition of their continuing significance, have been carefully and deliberately incorporated into newer ones.

Geomagnetic image across the ramparts at the south side of Ráith na Ríg. It shows an entrance gap in the palisade and the unbroken (black) line of the ditch passing in front of it, demonstrating that there was no entrance here originally. The technique is designed to record and map tiny variations in the earth's magnetic field which can be caused by man-made features such as walls or ditches.

A stone pillar in the centre of the Forrad is reputed to be the **Lia Fáil**. It is clear from its phallic shape that it is a fertility symbol and this concords well with the role ascribed to it in the description of the inauguration ceremony. It was moved here from its original position near the Mound of the Hostages to mark the grave of those who fell in the 1798 rebellion and had a small cross and the letters RIP carved into it. It is white granite and may have been quarried from outcrops in the north of Ireland, the nearest source being at Newry, County Down.

Ditch

Palisade
Trench

Ring Ditch

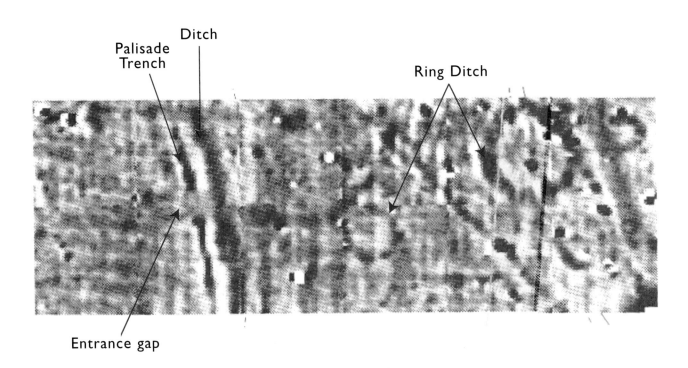

Entrance gap

The Rath of the Synods.

THE RATH OF THE SYNODS was thus named to commemorate ecclesiastical synods reputed to have been held at Tara by Adomnán, abbot of Iona (died 704).

Large parts of the site were destroyed between 1899 and 1902 by the British Israelites whose researches led them to believe that the Ark of the Covenant had been buried there.

Scientific excavations were carried out on the site in 1952 and 1953 and four major phases of activity were identified.

During the first phase the site was a burial ground consisting of an oval-shaped enclosure (27.5m by 32m) defined simply by a ditch, corresponding roughly to the central area of the present ringfort, and a small ring-barrow to the northwest, now tucked between the middle and outer ramparts. There is only circumstantial evidence that these two

One of the ditches at the Rath of the Synods as uncovered by the British Israelites (c. 1900).

features should be linked together. In its original form the barrow (about 17m in diameter) consisted of a cairn of stones covered by a mantle of soil thrown up from the excavation of the ditch. There were five primary cremation burials in the mound. Later, however, the top of the mound was levelled and spread out creating a wider but slighter monument. Five burials are associated with this phase, four cremations and one crouched inhumation which was placed over the centre of the mound. There were no associated artefacts and the time interval between the two stages cannot be ascertained.

The second phase is characterised by a series of palisaded enclosures ranging in diameter from about 16m to about 30m. These too coincide with the central area of the later ringfort. At least four distinct building episodes are attested, including the erection of at least one circle of free-standing wooden posts. The design and layout of these structures compare well with ritual and high status buildings at Dún Ailinne and Emain Macha which have been dated by excavation to the Iron Age and this suggests that they share a common, ceremonial purpose. A layer of sterile yellow soil seals these deposits and marks the end of this phase of activity.

During the third phase the site was once again used as a cemetery. We do not know if the area was formally defined, but there was a cluster of seven burials consisting of five inhumations and just two cremations. The proportionately greater number of inhumations reflects a gradual change in the burial rite from cremation to inhumation that took place during the first few centuries after the birth of Christ.

The building of a ringfort (83m in diameter) represents the fourth phase of activity. It is one of the very rare examples with four sets of ramparts. Others include Tlachtga on the Hill of Ward, a little to the west of Tara, and Rathra near Crúachain, County Roscommon. Like the Rath of the Synods, these too surround earlier burial mounds and it is clear that between them they constitute a special class of ritual or

Photo: Courtesy National Museum of Ireland

ceremonial monuments. The inner enclosure appears to have been aligned on the phase one ditched enclosure and the ringfort was positioned so as to facilitate the incorporation of the ring-barrow between the outer two ramparts. Each rampart consists of a bank and external ditch which, though substantially silted over today, originally attained depths of between 1.5 and 2m. The inner faces of the outer two banks may have been timber-faced. Remains of two rectangular buildings were found in the interior and the range of associated artefacts suggest that the site was occupied during the period 300 – 500 AD. Direct contact with the Roman world (probably Roman Britain) is also evidenced in the assemblage which includes objects such as a lead seal, a layered glass inset for a ring or brooch and an iron barrel padlock.

THE TECH MIDCHÚARTA or Banqueting Hall at Tara so captured the imagination of the medieval men of learning that they composed fanciful descriptions and illustrations of the king's court there. They imagined that the monument consisted of a hall, with seven opposed doorways, at the top of which the king of Tara presided over his court, each member being designated a place according to rank. Its heyday was supposed to have occurred during the reign of Cormac mac Airt, whose court was said to have been surpassed only by that of Solomon, son of David.

The monument is a linear earthwork consisting of two parallel, though slightly curved banks running downslope from south to north for a distance of 203m. There are slight traces of a terminal bank across the south end. Material for the bank appears to have been

Tech Midchúarta (the Banqueting Hall).

derived from the central area which had been dug out to below the surrounding ground level. There are five gaps in the west bank and two slight depressions near the south end. It is more difficult to see the original gaps along the east bank because they were deliberately filled in when a ditch was dug along its base. Five, or possibly six gaps can, however, be noted. But for some quarrying at the north end which foreshortened the east bank, the monument appears to survive to its original length. The north end may originally have terminated in an area of boggy ground known in the *dinnshenchas* as *Sescend Temrach* ('The Marsh of Tara').

Irish linear earthworks can be divided broadly between those that act as boundary markers or defensive frontiers, of which there is a fine example at least 1.5km long to the west of Tara, and those that appear to have been built for ceremonial or ritual purposes such as the Mucklaghs at Crúachain, County Roscommon and the Knockauns at Teltown, County Meath. The only available dating evidence in Ireland is for the boundary markers, which seem to have been built in the centuries around the birth of Christ. What the Tech Midchúarta has in common with ritual linear earthworks apart from its location, is its curvature, the multitude of gaps and the possibility that one end terminates in an area of boggy ground. These monuments may have been built as symbolic representations of

Socketed bronze axehead from Corballis, near Tara.

functioning boundary markers. Another possibility is that the Tech Midchúarta is a cursus monument. Cursus monuments, sometimes described as ceremonial avenues, are characteristic of the Middle to Late Neolithic in Britain and are an integral part of developed ritual landscapes, three occuring around Stonehenge in Wiltshire. They are exceptionally rare in Ireland – a possible variant occurs near Newgrange, County Meath. They are often aligned on earlier ritual and burial monuments and sometimes played an important role in the subsequent spatial development of ritual monuments. The alignment of the Tech Midchúarta on the Mound of the Hostages is evidence in support of its being described as a cursus.

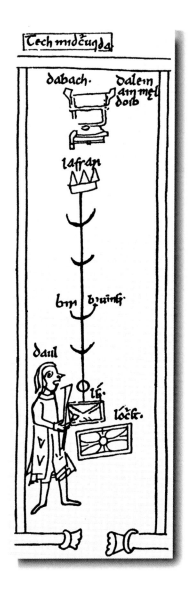

Detail of the plan of the Tech Midchúarta from the twelfth-century manuscript, The Book of Leinster. (After O'Ríordáin, S.P. 1965).

Ráith Gráinne is named after the legendary princess Gráinne, who fled from Tara and from Finn mac Cumaill with her lover Diarmait úa Duibne. It is a barrow (about 60m in diameter) consisting of a central mound surrounded by a ditch and external bank. In the centre are the remains of what may be another, small barrow. By combining geophysical and topographic data it has been possible to demonstrate that the slight prominence in the northeastern side is actually the central burial mound of an earlier ring-barrow that was incorporated into Ráith Gráinne. It too encompasses a small barrow into its northeastern quadrant suggesting that this was an accepted custom at the time.

Ráith Gráinne.

To the northeast of Ráith Gráinne are the remains of up to four extremely low-profile sites which can be seen when the sun is low on the western horizon.

The shape of the monument known as the **CLÓENFHERTA**, the 'Sloping Trenches', gave rise to a number of early tales. They were regarded as the remnants of the royal residence which collapsed when the king of Tara, Lugaid mac Con gave a false judgement. A second explanation for the shape of the monument is that it was the burial place of thirty princesses from Leinster slain by the king of Tara in revenge for the actions of the king of Leinster. These two monuments are ring-barrows that have been built on the edge of the steeply sloping western flank of the hill. In spite of the difficulty of digging a bank and ditch on so steep a gradient, both form complete circles and this supports the view that it was important to complete the circuit to comply with ritual convention. At over 80m in diameter, the northern site is by far the largest barrow at Tara. A hole was dug into the central mound, possibly by treasure hunters. The keen observer can make out the remains of a smaller barrow incorporated into the bank at the north side of the site.

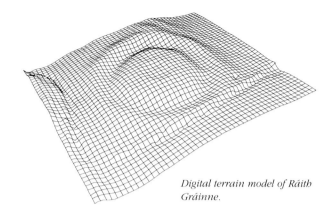

Digital terrain model of Ráith Gráinne.

Hill Shaded model.

Resistivity Survey.

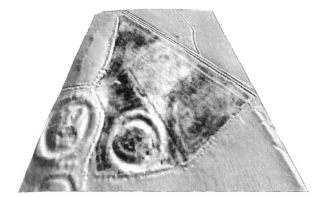

Geophysical and topographic survey of Ráith Gráinne.

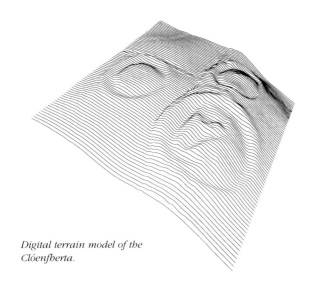

Digital terrain model of the Clóenfherta.

The southern of the Clóenfherta is about 48m in diameter. There is a small mound on top of the main mound. There are three further mounds tucked in between the northern and southern Clóenfherta and these too are probably burial monuments. South of this and along the crest of the ridge the remains of up to eight small, low barrows without banks can be identified.

The Clóenfherta.

Photo: Courtesy National Library of Ireland.

the Church

Engraving of the early church at Tara by Grose (1792).

From the late twelfth century onwards, Tara was one of the settlements which formed part of the Anglo-Norman kingdom of Meath. The land around Tara was held by the de Repenteni family, though early Anglo-Norman documents indicate that other families in the area, most particularly the de Feipo family of Skreen, contended with them for possession of Tara. This contention was part of the rivalry between King John and Walter de Lacy over the fertile and rich lands of the kingdom of Meath.

Ecclesiastical documents of the period provide the earliest references to the existence of a church at Tara. The church was associated with the Hospitallers of Saint John of Kilmainham, County Dublin. The

*The east window of the present church, **Pentecost** by Evie Hone (1936).*

Hospitallers' possessions, including the church at Tara, were confirmed to them by Pope Innocent III in 1212. It continued to function as a parish church until the sixteenth century, when it fell into disrepair. Bishop James Ussher, Protestant Archbishop of Dublin and distinguished scholar (1581–1656), visited Tara in 1622, and noted that 'the church and chauncell are altogether ruyned'. The medieval parish church was demolished in about 1823 and was replaced by the present church. A large block of masonry lying on its side in the graveyard is all that remains of the earlier building. Some of the finely dressed masonry, including the elaborate pointed arch window incorporated into the western facade of the church, was salvaged from the earlier one. A memorial to Sir Robert Dillon dating to 1595 is mounted on the wall inside the church and reads...

ROBERTUS DILLON DE REVERSTON MILES CAPLISIUST DNE ELI COIL BACI REGNI SUI HIBER AC UN DE P--VATO CONSILIO ET DN KATHERINA SARSFELD UXOR EI HOC OPUS FECERVT 7 OCTOB ADNII 1595

translated thus:

Robert Dillon of Riverstown, Soldier, Chief Justice of the common pleas to the Lady Elizabeth in her Kingdom of Ireland, also one of the Privy Council and the Lady Katherine Sarsfield his wife, erected this work 7th October 1595

There are two standing stones in the churchyard, one is tall and regularly shaped and is sometimes referred to as **ADOMNÁN'S CROSS**, the other a squat, rounded pillar. On the east side of the taller stone is a small, overtly sexual figure or sheela-na-gig carved in relief. Isolated examples of sheela-na-gigs can be extremely difficult to date owing to the fact that this type of carving has a very long ancestry as a pagan fertility symbol. In Ireland they are more commonly found built into the fabric of buildings such as churches and can, therefore, be dated to the medieval period. It is very unusual to find one on a free-standing stone such as at Tara and this leads one to suspect that this stone may once have been part of an earlier church.

Sheela-na-gig in the church grounds.

the artefacts

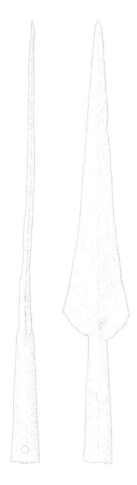

Iron spearhead from Ballinter, near Tara.

Apart from material discovered during the excavations of the Rath of the Synods and the Mound of the Hostages, only a handful of stray (or chance) finds are attributed to the Hill of Tara. This is all the more surprising given that in the past the commercial value of an artefact could be increased by falsely provenancing it to a well-known site such as Tara. Such, for example, is the case with the famous Tara Brooch which was actually found at Bettystown, near Drogheda, County Meath. The same may be true of a large block of red enamel that was found in 1857 near Kilmessan, a little to the west of Tara, and which may have been broken into two pieces, one now in the National Museum of Ireland, the other in the British Museum where it is described as having come from Tara. Thus, without satisfactory corroboration, it is impossible to verify the find circumstances of many of the stray artefacts. It is reasonably certain, however, that the two gold, bar-twisted torcs (neck-rings) reputed to have been found near the church in 1810 are genuinely from Tara (see Page 17). They are the largest and most elaborate of their type which are conventionally dated to the Middle Bronze Age (about 1200 BC). They may have been a votive offering.

Over half of the stray finds provenanced to Tara are of prehistoric date, early historic and medieval artefacts account for just a few. This trend is reflected in the thirty or so stray finds from an area of 100km^2 around the Hill of Tara, which include bronze axes, a sword and a spear of Late Bronze Age date and a decorated bridle bit and Y-shaped pendant dating to the Iron Age.

Scholars and Tara

Tara has attracted the attention of archaeologists and antiquarians for many generations. The medieval corpus of material known as *Dinnshenchas Érenn* could be regarded as an early topographical survey of parts of Ireland. It seeks to explain the origin and background to the names of the most prominent natural and man-made features in the country. Of all places which feature in the *dinnshenchas*, Tara is placed in a primary position. The names of the sites on Tara that are used today are taken from these texts. It is likely that the *dinnshenchas* accounts of Tara were composed in the tenth and eleventh centuries as part of a series of texts which helped to promote the cause of Máel Sechnaill II, Brian Ború's main rival.

In 1839 the antiquarian George Petrie published the first detailed survey of the legends and monuments of Tara. He supplemented the recently published Ordnance Survey map of Tara with monuments that had previously gone unnoticed and others whose position he extrapolated from detailed analysis of the *dinnshenchas*. In 1919, R.A.S. Macalister, the first professor of Celtic Archaeology in the National University of Ireland, published the second major account of the monuments at Tara. The emphasis in both of these surveys is placed on correlating and analysing the topographic and historical entries in the *dinnshenchas* and this approach has dominated all subsequent work on Tara.

In 1952, Professor Séan P. Ó Ríordáin embarked on an ambitious programme of research starting with two seasons of excavations (in 1952 and 1953) at the Rath of the Synods. Two further seasons of excavations were carried out by Ó Ríordáin at the Mound of the Hostages in 1955 and 1956 and they were completed in 1959 under the direction of Ruaidhrí de Valera, Ó Ríordáin's successor to the chair of Celtic archaeology at University College Dublin.

SUGGESTED FURTHER READING

Petrie, G. 1839 On the history and antiquities of Tara Hill. *Transactions of the Royal Irish Academy* **18**, 25-232.

Macalister, R.A.S. 1931 *Tara a pagan sanctuary of ancient Ireland.* London.

Ó Ríordáin, S.P. 1965 *Tara, the monuments on the hill.* Dundalk.

Byrne, F.J. 1969 *The rise of the Uí Néill and the high-kingship of Ireland.* (O'Donnell Lecture Series) Dublin.

Byrne, F.J. 1973 *Irish kings and high-kings.* London.

Raftery, B. 1994 *Pagan Celtic Ireland. The enigma of the Irish Iron Age.* London.

Bhreathnach, E. 1995 *Tara, a select bibliography.* Discovery Programme Report 3. Dublin.